# KEN HO.
# VEGETABLE &
# PASTA BOOK

Ken Hom is also the author of
*Illustrated Chinese Cookery,*
*Vegetarian Cookery*
*East Meets West*

ADAPTED AND EDITED BY Wendy Hobson
ILLUSTRATIONS BY Teresa O'Brien

Published by William Levene Ltd
167 Imperial Drive
Harrow Middlesex
England

First published 1994

This edition specially published by William Levene Limited
by arrangement with BBC Books
and not to be sold separately

ISBN 0 563 37096 3

# CONTENTS

# INTRODUCTION

*O*ne of the most exciting culinary developments in recent years has been the introduction into Western cuisine of a whole range of Chinese, Japanese and Southeast Asian methods and ingredients, especially the seasonings. Flavours that used to be 'exotic' are now well on their way to becoming standards in home cooking.

Each recipe in this book reflects my own tastes and preferences and is drawn from my own observations and experiences. The result is a very personal, eclectic collection which nevertheless has a unified theme: good food, especially vegetables and pasta, that is delicious, flavourful and easily prepared, with an oriental flair that blends congenially with a Western meal.

Growing up within the Chinese culinary tradition, fresh vegetables, noodles and pasta – wonderful foods – have been central to my diet in both my personal and professional life ever since I can remember. When I was a child, Chinese pasta (of which there are many types, shapes and sizes) and vegetables were as much a part of my diet as were rice and beancurd.

When I became old enough to venture out into the mainstream of Western culture, I was appalled by the way vegetables and pasta were cooked. I had always loved vegetables but I understood my schoolmates' aversion to them, overcooked as they were to the point of limpness and tastelessness. As for pasta, it was gummy and devoid of its customary textures and subtle tastes, overcooked and drowned in tomato sauce. I thought it all quite unnecessary.

In the Chinese cultural environment, food is a source of happiness for both body and soul: meal times are times of an almost religious sharing, of conversation and family interaction, with proper attention having been paid to the preparation of the foods. My mother prepared meat, fish and poultry dishes, but they never dominated our table. Rather, vegetables and pasta, with rice too, of course, were the mainstay of our diet. Vegetables, both Chinese and European varieties, were more important to us than meats. And I relished them, finding them flavourful, colourful and cooked to perfection. This means, among other things, that vegetables were preferably as fresh as possible and never overcooked – preserving their natural flavours and nutrients. So too were our noodle and pasta dishes, prepared so that they retained their textures and tastes and were never overwhelmed by any sauce.

I agree with a food critic who wrote that the phrase *al dente* is both overworked and vague; the only workable test of doneness for both vegetables and pasta is the 'nibble test'. Be prepared to nibble or taste your foods during preparation, as only you can tell when they are ready.

I must emphasise that this is *not* a vegetarian cookbook, although it can be used very usefully by vegetarians. Many of the recipes in this book can accompany other dishes, oriental or not, vegetarian or not, for lunch, dinner or supper. As such, the recipes embody the ideas, tastes, flavours, colours, aromas and aesthetics inspired by my own dual Asian–Western tradition. You may, if you wish, add meat or poultry to some of the recipes – whatever your own taste tells you is appropriate. Experiment with the recipes to make them your own. I can only be a guide on your first steps into this delightful terrain. Your taste and imagination, with loving care in your preparations, will take you much further than any guide could ever do. Happy cooking and eating!

# INGREDIENTS

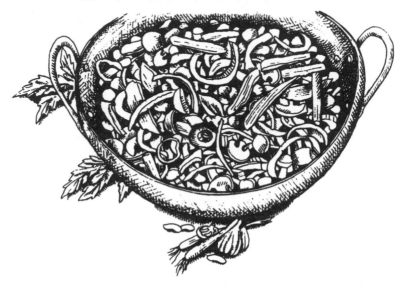

*F*resh vegetables are, of course, essential to good cooking. But equally important are the other ingredients – the seasonings, spices and sauces that complement and enhance the virtues of the vegetables. The recipes in this book draw upon a number of special ingredients which give a distinctive taste to the vegetables and pasta, making them authentic versions of the Chinese, Japanese and Southeast Asian originals.

## BAMBOO SHOOTS

Bamboo shoots are the young edible shoots of certain kinds of bamboo. In Britain, they are only available tinned. Pale yellow with a crunchy texture, they come peeled and either whole or thickly sliced. Rinse them thoroughly before use and transfer any remaining shoots to a jar, cover them with fresh water and keep in the refrigerator. If the water is changed daily they will keep for up to a week.

## BEANCURD

Beancurd is also known by its Chinese name, 'doufu', or by its Japanese name, 'tofu'. It is highly nutritious, being rich in protein, and combines well with other foods. Beancurd has a distinctive texture but a bland taste. It is made from yellow soya beans which are soaked, ground, mixed with water and then cooked briefly before being solidified. In Britain, it is usually sold in two forms, firm cakes or as a thickish junket, but it is also available in several dried forms and fermented.

## BEAN SPROUTS

Bean sprouts are the sprouts of the green mung bean. Bean sprouts should always be very fresh and crunchy. They will keep for several days wrapped in a plastic bag and stored in the vegetable compartment of a refrigerator. Tinned bean sprouts are soggy and tasteless.

## BLACK BEANS

These small black soya beans, also known as salted black beans, are pre-served by being fermented with salt and spices. They have a distinctive, slightly salty taste and a pleasantly rich smell, and are used as a seasoning, often in conjunction with garlic and fresh ginger. Black beans are inexpensive and can be obtained in tins, as 'black beans in salted sauce'; you may also see them packed in plastic bags, which are preferable. Rinse before use; I prefer to chop the beans slightly too. Transfer any unused beans and liquid to a sealed jar and they keep indefinitely if stored in the refrigerator.

## CHILLIES

Chillies are used extensively in western China and somewhat less frequently in the south, as well as many parts of Southeast Asia. They are the seed pods of the capsicum plant and can be obtained fresh, dried or ground.

Fresh chillies Fresh chillies can be distinguished by their small size and elongated shape. They should look fresh and bright with no brown patches or black spots. Red chillies are generally milder than green ones.

To prepare fresh chillies, first rinse them in cold water. Slit them lengthways and remove and discard the seeds. Rinse well under cold running water, and then prepare according to the recipe. Wash your hands, knife and board before preparing other foods, and be careful not to touch your eyes until you have washed your hands thoroughly with soap and water.

Dried red chillies Dried red chillies are small and thin, and about 1 cm (½ in) long. They are used to season oil for stir-fried dishes, sauces and for braising. They are normally left whole or cut in half.

Chilli powder, Chilli powder, also known as cayenne pepper, is made from ground dried red chillies. It is pungent and ranges from hot to very hot.

## CHINESE LEAVES

Chinese leaves (*Brassica pekinensis*) look rather like a large, tightly packed cos lettuce with firm, pale green, crinkled leaves. It is sometimes known as Chinese or Peking cabbage. It is a delicious crunchy vegetable with a mild but distinctive taste. If you cannot find it, use English white cabbage instead.

## CINNAMON STICKS/BARK

Cinnamon sticks are curled, paper-thin pieces of the bark of the cinnamon tree. They add a robust taste to braised dishes and are an important ingredient of five spice powder. Ground cinnamon is not a satisfactory substitute.

## COCONUT MILK

Tinned coconut milk is available in supermarkets. Look for the ones from Thailand and Malaysia. Shake the tins well before opening. Any remainder can be kept in the refrigerator for at least a week out of the tin.

## CORIANDER (CHINESE PARSLEY)

Fresh coriander is one of the relatively few herbs used in Chinese cookery. It looks like flat parsley but its pungent, musky, citrus-like flavour gives it a distinctive and unmistakable character. Its feathery leaves are often used as a garnish or it can be chopped and then mixed into sauces and stuffings. Parsley may be used as a substitute.

To store coriander, wash in cold water, drain thoroughly and put it in a clean polythene bag with a couple of sheets of moist kitchen paper. Stored in the vegetable compartment of the refrigerator, it should keep for several days.

## FIVE SPICE POWDER

Five spice powder is a mixture of star anise, Sichuan peppercorns, fennel, cloves and cinnamon. A good blend is pungent, fragrant, spicy and slightly sweet at the same time.

## GINGER

Fresh root ginger (actually a rhizome, not a root) is indispensable in oriental cookery. Its pungent, spicy and fresh taste adds a subtle but distinctive flavour to soups, meats, fish, sauces and vegetables. Fresh ginger looks rather like a gnarled Jerusalem artichoke. It has pale brown, dry skin which is usually peeled away before use. Select fresh ginger which is firm with no signs of shrivelling. It will keep in the refrigerator, well wrapped in cling film, for up to 2 weeks. Dried powdered ginger has a quite different flavour and cannot be substituted for fresh ginger.

## MUSHROOMS, CHINESE DRIED

There are many varieties of these which add a particular flavour and aroma to Chinese dishes. These mushrooms can be black or brown in colour. The very large ones, with a lighter colour and a highly cracked surface, are the best and so they are usually the most expensive. Keep them stored in an airtight jar in a cool dry place.

To use Chinese dried mushrooms, soak the required amount in hot water for about 20 minutes until soft. Squeeze out any excess liquid and remove the tough, inedible stalk. The resulting liquid can be used for cooking rice – simply pour off the liquid gently, leaving any residue behind.

Chinese dried cloud ears (black fungus) and wood ears These tiny dried mushrooms are soaked in hot water for 20–30 minutes until soft. Rinse well and cut away any hard pieces. They are valued for their crunchy texture and slightly smokey flavour. Wood ears are the larger variety.

## NOODLES

Wheat and egg noodles These are made from hard or soft wheat flour and water. If egg has been added, the noodles are usually labelled as egg noodles. They can be bought dried or fresh. Flat noodles are usually used in soups, and rounded noodles are best for stir-frying. If you can't get Chinese noodles, you can use Italian egg noodles instead.

To cook wheat and egg noodles, immerse them in a saucepan of boiling water and cook for 3–5 minutes or until they are soft. Drain and serve.

If you are cooking noodles ahead of time before using them in another dish or before stir-frying them, toss the cooked drained noodles in a teaspoon or two of sesame oil and put them into a bowl. Cover this with cling film and put it in the refrigerator for up to 2 hours.

Rice noodles Rice noodles are white and come in a variety of shapes. One of the most common is rice stick noodles, which are flat and about the length of a chopstick. Simply soak them in warm water for 15 minutes or until they are soft. Drain them and use in soups or stir-fries.

Bean thread (transparent) noodles These noodles, also called cellophane noodles, are made from ground mung beans. They are available dried, and are very fine and white. They are never served on their own, but are added to soups or braised dishes or are deep-fried as a garnish. They must be soaked in warm water for about 5 minutes before use. As they are rather long, you might find it easier to cut them into shorter lengths after soaking. They can also be fried, in which case do not soak them before use.

## OILS

Oil is the most commonly used cooking medium in the East. The favourite is groundnut (peanut) oil, although you can use corn or vegetable oil.

I find oils are best re-used just once or twice, this is healthier since constantly re-using oils increases the saturated fat content. To prepare oil for re-use, simply cook the oil after use and filter it through muslin or a fine strainer into a jar. Cover tightly and keep in a cool, dry place.

Sesame oil This is a thick, rich, golden brown oil made from sesame seeds, which has a distinctive, nutty flavour and aroma. It is widely used in Chinese and Japanese cookery as a seasoning.

Chilli oil Chilli oil is too dramatic to be used directly in cooking; it is best applied as a final spicy touch.

## PEANUTS

Raw peanuts are used in oriental cooking to add flavour and a crunchy texture. The thin red skins need to be removed before you use the nuts. To do this, simply immerse them in a pan of boiling water for about 2 minutes. Drain, leave to cool and the skins will come off easily.

## RICE

Long-grain This is the most popular rice for Asian food and is my own favourite, too. Do not confuse it with the 'easy-cook' and other pre-cooked varieties which are widely available.

Washing rice is optional. Put the required amount of rice into a large bowl, fill it with cold water and swish the rice around with your hands. Carefully pour off the cloudy water, keeping the rice in the bowl. Repeat several times until the water is clear.

To cook long-grain rice, fill a glass measuring jug with long-grain rice to the 450 ml (15 fl oz) level.

Put the rice into a large bowl and wash it if you wish. Drain the rice and put it into a heavy pan with 900 ml (1½ pints) of water and bring to the boil. Continue boiling for 15–20 minutes until most of the surface liquid has evaporated. The surface of the rice should have small indentations like a pitted crater. At this point, cover the pan with a *very* tight-fitting lid, turn the heat as low as possible and let the rice cook undisturbed for 15–20 minutes.

Short grain This rice is not to be confused with pudding rice. Short-grain is slightly stickier than long-grain white rice, but is cooked in the same way.

Glutinous Glutinous rice is also known as sweet or sticky rice. It is short, round and pearl-like, and is not to be confused with ordinary short-grain or pudding rice. It is used for substantial rice dishes such as Steamed Sticky Rice, or in stuffings, desserts and for making Chinese rice wine and vinegar. Glutinous rice must be soaked for at least 2 hours (preferably overnight) before cooking in the same way as long-grain rice.

## RICE WINE

This wine is used extensively for cooking and drinking throughout China. It is made from glutinous rice, yeast and spring water. A good quality, dry pale sherry can be substituted but cannot equal the rich, mellow taste of Chinese rice wine.

## SAUCES AND PASTES

Tinned sauces, once opened, should be transferred to screw-top glass jars and kept in the refrigerator, where they will last for a long time.

Chilli bean sauce This is a thick dark sauce or paste made from soya beans, chillies and other seasonings, and is very hot and spicy.

Chilli sauce Chilli sauce is a hot, bright red sauce made from chillies, vinegar, sugar and salt. It is sometimes used for cooking, but is mainly used as a dipping sauce. If you find it too strong, dilute with hot water.

Curry paste This prepared paste has a stronger curry flavour than the powdered variety. The spices are mixed with oil and chilli peppers. Be sure to get the Indian variety which is generally the best. Kept refrigerated.

Dipping sauces and mixtures Many Chinese and Southeast Asian dishes and snacks are dipped into a variety of dipping sauces before being eaten. The most popular of these are chilli sauce and chilli oil. Soy sauces and red and black Chinese rice vinegars are also used as dips.

Fish sauce Fish sauce, also known as fish gravy or 'nam pla', is a thin brownish sauce made from fermented salted fresh fish. It is sold bottled and has a very fish odour and salty taste. Cooking greatly diminishes the 'fishy' flavour and the sauce adds a subtle taste to many dishes.

Hoisin sauce This is a thick, dark, brownish red sauce, made from soya beans, vinegar, sugar, spices and other flavourings. It is sweet and spicy and is widely used in southern Chinese cookery. Keep refrigerated.

Oyster sauce This thin brown sauce is made from a concentrate of oysters cooked in soy sauce and brine. Oyster sauce has a rich flavour and is used not only in cooking but also as a condiment, diluted with a little oil, for vegetables, poultry or meats. It keeps best in the refrigerator.

Sesame paste This rich, thick, creamy brown paste is made from sesame seeds. It is used in both hot and cold dishes, and is particularly popular in northern and western China. If you cannot obtain it, use peanut butter.

## SOY SAUCES

Soy sauce is made from a mixture of soya beans, flour and water, which is then naturally fermented and matured for some months. The liquid which is finally distilled is soy sauce. There are two main types, light and dark.

Light soy sauce As the name implies, this is light in colour but it is full of flavour and is the best one to use for cooking. It is saltier than dark soy sauce. In Chinese grocers, light soy sauce is known as Superior Soy.

Dark soy sauce This sauce is matured for much longer than light soy sauce, hence its darker, almost black, colour. Slightly thicker and stronger than light soy sauce, it is more suitable for stews. I prefer it to light soy sauce as a dipping sauce. It is known in Chinese grocers as Soy Superior Sauce.

Yellow bean sauce This thick, spicy, aromatic sauce is made with yellow beans, flour and salt which are fermented together. It is quite salty but adds a distinctive flavour to Chinese sauces. There are two forms: whole beans in a thick sauce or mashed or puréed beans (sold as crushed yellow bean sauce). It keeps best in the refrigerator.

## SESAME SEEDS

These are dried seeds of an oriental annual herb. Sesame seeds are valued as a flavouring agent and as a source of oil and paste. Kept in a glass jar in a cool dry place, they will last indefinitely.

To toast sesame seeds, preheat the oven to 170°C/325°F/Gas 3. Spread the sesame seeds on a baking try. Roast them in the oven for about 10–15 minutes until they are lightly browned.

## SICHUAN PEPPERCORNS

Sichuan peppercorns are known throughout China as 'flower peppers' because they look like flower buds opening. They are reddish brown in colour with a strong pungent odour, which distinguishes them from the hotter black peppercorns. Sichuan peppercorns are not from peppers at all, but are the dried berries of a shrub which is a member of the citrus family. I find their smell reminds me of lavender, while their taste is sharp and mildly spicy. They can be ground in a conventional peppermill and are very often roasted in a dry frying pan before grinding to bring out their full flavour.

## STAR ANISE

This hard, star-shaped seed pod is similar to common aniseed but stronger. It is an essential ingredient in five-spice powder and widely used in braised dishes.

## VINEGARS

Chinese vinegars are usually made from rice and there are many varieties. If you cannot buy them, use cider vinegar.

## WATER CHESTNUTS

Fresh waterchestnuts will keep unpeeled in a paper bag in the refrigerator for 2 weeks. Look for a firm, hard texture. If you cannot find fresh ones, use tinned and rinse in cold water before using.

# EQUIPMENT AND TECHNIQUES

*T*he true tastes and flavours of China can only be achieved by using the appropriate cooking techniques, and proper technique requires proper equipment. While not absolutely essential for cooking Chinese food, there are a few items which will make it easier. Most are inexpensive, easily available and all are serviceable over a long period of time.

The most useful piece of equipment is the wok. It can be used for many types of cooking such as braising and deep-frying, and is particularly useful for cooking bulky vegetables like spinach, or to cook large quantities of food. It is best known, of course, as the ideal pan for stir-frying as it allows you to move the food around quickly without spilling it all over the place, and its shape spreads the heat evenly over the surface, thus making for the rapid cooking which is fundamental to stir-frying. When used for deep-frying, the smaller base of the wok requires less oil, but still provides the depth which is important to that technique.

In China most homes have round-bottomed woks which are set on top of charcoal braziers in which wood or charcoal is burnt to produce the high heat so important for Chinese cooking. The purpose of the traditional design is to concentrate intense heat at the centre, but living outside a Chinese kitchen requires some adjustment.

## CHOOSING A WOK

Choose a medium-sized wok with deep sides, a long handle and a slightly flat bottom. Some woks on the market are too shallow or too flat at the bottom, making them no better than a large frying pan or skillet. Select one which has heft to it, is not too light. These tend to scorch and do not withstand the high temperatures required for this type of cooking.

## PREPARING AND SEASONING THE WOK

Before using a wok, clean off the manufacturer's protective coating from inside. This will not cause any harm, but might taint the taste of food.

The easiest way to clean the bowl is to place the wok on the stove and heat it gently to soften the coating. Then scrub the bowl vigorously with a stiff pan brush or scouring pad until all the coating is removed.

Once the bowl is free of coating, it should be washed well and then dried. The final drying, to remove moisture from the pores of the metal, can be done by placing the wok back on the hob to heat for a minute or two on a medium heat. The wok is then ready for seasoning.

Rub the entire inner surface of the wok with a thick coating of corn or vegetable oil. Heat the wok gently until the oil smokes, then remove the wok from the heat and leave it until cold. Wipe off the excess oil with absorbent kitchen paper. Repeat the process two or three times. With continual use and seasoning, your wok will eventually become quite dark in colour and this will enhance the condition of the bowl.

Do not scrub a seasoned wok, just wash it in plain water without detergent. Dry it thoroughly, preferably by putting it over a low heat for a few minutes before putting it away. This should prevent the wok from rusting, but if it does, scrub off any rust with kitchen cleanser and repeat the seasoning process. You can rub the inside with cooking oil before storing.

## WOK ACCESSORIES

A wok stand is a metal ring or frame designed to keep a conventionally shaped wok steady when you are steaming, deep-frying or braising.

A wok lid is a dome-like cover, usually made from aluminium, which is used for steaming. It may come with the wok or it can be purchased separately, but any snugly fitting domed lid can be used instead.

A long-handled metal spatula shaped like a small shovel is ideal for tossing food in a wok. Any long-handled spoon can be used instead.

## OTHER EQUIPMENT

No self-respecting Chinese or Southeast Asian cook would been seen with a knife instead of a cleaver. These heavy choppers are used for all kinds of cutting, ranging from fine shredding to chopping up bones. Of course, you can prepare Chinese food using good sharp knives, but if you decide to invest in a cleaver, you will be surprised at how easy it is to use. Choose a good quality stainless steel one and keep it sharp.

The Chinese traditionally use a soft wood block for chopping, but I prefer to use a large, steady hardwood or acrylic board. (For health reasons never cut cooked meat on a board which you have used for chopping raw meat or poultry. Keep a separate board for this.) Always clean your cutting boards properly after use. Vinegar or lemon work well.

Bamboo steamers are round 'boxes' in several sizes. Bamboo steamers are filled with food and placed on top of a pan or over a wok of boiling water and tightly covered. One of the advantages of the design is that several steamers can be stacked on top of the other for multiple cooking. Before using a bamboo steamer for the first time, wash and steam it empty for about 5 minutes.

Chopsticks are not just used for eating in Chinese and Southeast Asian cooking (with the exception of Thais, who use forks). They are also used when cooking, for stirring, beating and whipping. Special long chopsticks are available for these purposes, but it is perfectly all right to use Western cooking implements instead.

## FOOD PREPARATION

The preparation of food before cooking is probably more important and more time-consuming in oriental cookery than in any other cuisine. It is important to have all ingredients properly prepared beforehand. In stir-frying, for example, the food must be chopped into small, well-shaped pieces. This will ensure even and quick cooking, and is especially important for vegetables so as to avoid overcooking. Foods prepared and cooked this way retain their natural textures and tastes, and visual appeal.

## COOKING TECHNIQUES

Chinese cookery is a sophisticated cuisine which involves a number of cooking methods which are relatively uncommon in the West. Sometimes several different cooking techniques are used in the preparation of a single dish, such as deep-frying bean-curd and then braising it.

Blanching   Blanching in water is common with harder vegetables such as broccoli or carrots. The vegetable is plunged into boiling water for several minutes. It is then drained and plunged into cold water to arrest the cooking process. In such cases, blanching usually precedes stir-frying which completes the cooking.

Poaching   This is a method of simmering food until it is partially cooked. It is then put into soup or combined with a sauce and the cooking process continued.

Stir-frying   This is the most famous of all Chinese cooking techniques and is used extensively. Success with it depends upon having all the required ingredients prepared, measured out and immediately to hand, and on having a good source of fierce heat. Its advantage is that, properly executed, stir-fried foods can be cooked in minutes in very little oil so they retain their natural flavours and textures. It is very important that stir-fried foods should not be overcooked or greasy. Once you have mastered this technique you will find that it becomes almost second nature. Using a wok is definitely an advantage when stir-frying as its shape not only conducts the heat well but its high sides enable you to toss and stir ingredients rapidly, keeping them constantly moving while cooking. Having prepared all the ingredients for stir-frying, follow the steps below.

Heat the wok or frying-pan until it is very hot *before* adding the oil. This prevents food sticking and will ensure an even heat. Add the oil and, using a metal spatula or long-handled spoon, distribute it evenly over the surface. It should be very hot indeed – almost smoking – before you add the next ingredient unless you are going on to flavour the oil (see next point).

If you are flavouring the oil with garlic, spring onions, ginger, dried red chilli or other seasoning, do not wait for the oil to get so hot that it is almost smoking. If you do, these ingredients will burn and become bitter. Toss them quickly in the oil for a few seconds. In some recipes these flavourings will then be removed and discarded before cooking proceeds.

Now add the ingredients as described in the recipe and proceed to stir-fry by tossing them over the surface of the wok or pan from the centre of the wok to the sides.

Some stir-fried dishes are thickened with a mixture of cornflour and cold water. To avoid getting a lumpy sauce be sure to remove the wok or pan from the heat before you add the cornflour mixture, which must be thoroughly blended before it is added. The sauce can then be returned to the heat and thickened.

Deep-frying This is one of the most important techniques in Chinese cookery. The trick is to regulate the heat so that the surface of the food is sealed but does not brown so fast that the food is uncooked inside. Although a deep-fried food must not be greasy, the process does require a lot of oil. Be sure that your wok, pan or deep-fat fryer is fully secure before adding the oil and on no account leave the wok unsupervised.

Wait for the oil to get hot enough before adding the food to be fried. The oil should give off a haze and almost produce little wisps of smoke when it is the right temperature, but you can test it by dropping in a small piece of food. If it bubbles all over then the oil is sufficiently hot. Adjust the heat as necessary to prevent the oil from actually smoking or overheating.

Be sure to dry food to be deep-fried thoroughly first with kitchen paper as this will prevent spluttering. If the food is in a marinade, remove it with a slotted spoon and drain before putting it into the oil. If you are using batter, make sure all the excess batter drips off before adding the food to the hot oil.

Shallow-frying or pan-frying This technique is similar to sautéeing. It involves more oil that stir-frying but less than for deep-frying. Food is fried first on one side and then on the other. Sometimes the excess oil is drained off and a sauce added to complete the dish.

Slow-simmering and steeping In slow-simmering, food is immersed in liquid which is brought almost to the boil and then the temperature is reduced so that it simmers, cooking the food to the desired degree. In steeping, food is similarly immersed in liquid (usually stock) and simmered for a time. The heat is then turned off and the residual heat of the liquid finishes off the cooking process.

Braising These techniques are most often applied to certain vegetables. The food is usually browned or deep-fried and then put into stock which has been flavoured with seasonings and spices. The stock is brought to the boil, the heat reduced and the food simmered gently until it is cooked.

Steaming Steaming has been used by the Chinese for thousands of years. Steamed foods are cooked by a gentle moist heat which must circulate freely in order to cook the food. It is an excellent method for bringing out subtle flavours and so is particularly good for fish. Food to be steamed should be placed on a heatproof plate on a rack or in a steamer about 2.5 cm (1 in) about 5 cm (2 in) of simmering water in a covered wok or pan.

# STARTERS AND SIDE DISHES

*S*tarters are meant to stimulate the palate, to prepare one for the offerings to come. As such, I like them to be subtly appealing in taste and textures. In most cases they should be simple and light, for you don't wish to overwhelm the main course. The rule here is to make and use the recipes as they fit into your meal or menu. They may be used as starters; as a first course in a series of courses; or as a part of many courses – that is, if you wish to follow the Chinese custom of including different courses on the table at once; or you may serve them as another dish in a family meal. Use these starters with all styles of cookery, not just Chinese. Be imaginative – combine or match these appetisers with other foods and beverages, or serve them as snacks or mini meals in themselves.

# HOT AND SPICY WALNUTS

*T*his is a spicy, savoury way to prepare walnuts to be served either as a snack with drinks or as a crunchy addition to other stir-fry dishes. Prepared this way, the walnuts lend themselves to many uses; use your imagination and experiment with them. If the walnuts get soft before they are used, you may recrisp them by heating in a warm oven. They can be made ahead of time but should be eaten within a few days of their preparation. They do not keep for a long time because of the seasonings used in this recipe.

SERVES 4

225 g (8 oz) walnuts, shelled
2 tablespoons chilli bean sauce
1 tablespoon finely chopped garlic
1 tablespoon finely chopped fresh ginger
3 tablespoons Chinese black rice vinegar or cider vinegar

2 tablespoons sugar
2 tablespoons dark soy sauce
2 tablespoons Chinese white rice vinegar or cider vinegar
700 ml (1¼ pints) water
400 ml (15 fl oz) oil (preferably groundnut), for deep-frying

GARNISH

3 tablespoons finely chopped spring onions

Bring a pan of water to the boil. Add the walnuts and simmer for about 5 minutes to blanch. Drain the nuts in a colander or sieve, then pat dry with kitchen paper.

Combine all the remaining ingredients together in a wok or pan. Add the walnuts and cook for about 20 minutes over high heat. Drain the nuts and spread them on a baking tray. Leave to dry for at least 2 hours or more.

Heat the oil in a wok or deep-fat fryer to a moderate heat. Fry some of the walnuts for about 3 minutes or until they turn deep brown and crispy. (Watch the heat to prevent burning.) You may have to deep-fry them in several batches. Remove the walnuts with a slotted spoon or strainer and drain on kitchen paper. Allow them to cool and become crisp before serving. Garnish with the spring onions.

# WINTER VEGETABLE FRITTERS

These vegetable fritters (similar to pancakes), served warm or at room temperature, are an appetising starter for any meal. You may substitute other vegetables as long as they are firm, such as cucumbers or courgettes. Served with a simple green salad, these vegetable fritters also make a delicious light lunch.

SERVES 2–4

100 g (4 oz) carrots
100 g (4 oz) fresh or tinned
  waterchestnuts
100 g (4 oz) cabbage
1 small onion
6 tablespoons plain flour
1 tablespoon cornflour
3 eggs, beaten

2 teaspoons salt
2 teaspoons baking powder
2 teaspoons sugar
1 teaspoon freshly ground black
  pepper
3–4 tablespoons oil (preferably
  groundnut)

Finely chop the carrots, waterchestnuts, cabbage and onion. Lightly blend all the ingredients, except the oil, in a food processor or food mill for a few seconds. Do not use a blender.

Heat a wok or frying-pan and add the oil. Spoon in 3 tablespoons of the mixture to make a 10 cm (4 in) wide pancake and fry for 2–3 minutes or until golden brown on one side. Using a knife or spatula, turn the pancake over and cook the other side until crispy and golden. Continue this process until you have used up all the mixture. Cut the fritters into wedges and serve.

# COLD GREEN BEAN SALAD

*S*implicity itself, this recipe takes a favourite vegetable and gives it a touch of Southeast Asian zest. The fish sauce is commonly used in many parts of Southeast Asia and, when combined with other spices, will enliven any dish. Serve these beans either as a salad or as a side vegetable dish. They may be prepared well ahead of time.

SERVES 2–4

225 g (8 oz) runner or French
    beans, trimmed
1 tablespoon oil (preferably
    groundnut)
1 small onion, finely chopped

DRESSING

1 tablespoon fish sauce
2 tablespoons sesame seeds,
    toasted
2 tablespoons lemon juice

2 teaspoons sesame oil
1 teaspoon salt
2 teaspoons chilli oil

If you are using runner beans, cut them into 7.5 cm (3 in) lengths. If you are using French beans, leave whole. Blanch the beans in a large pan of boiling salted water for 2 minutes. Immerse them in cold water, drain thoroughly and set aside.

Heat a wok or frying-pan and add the oil. When moderately hot, add the onion and stir-fry for 2 minutes, then allow to cool. Add to the beans.

Combine all the dressing ingredients and toss with the beans and onion. Serve the salad immediately or refrigerate and serve the next day.

# ASPARAGUS WITH TANGY MUSTARD DRESSING

Asparagus is a relative newcomer to the cast of vegetables in oriental cuisine, but there is no doubt it has won a permanent starring role in the repertoire. Its popularity is based on contrasts: properly cooked, it has a firm but soft texture, a delicate yet earthy assertive flavour – and a brilliant colour. In this Japanese-style recipe, the asparagus is simply cooked by quickly blanching, the briefest processing possible. The mustard-ginger dressing only highlights and never intrudes upon the taste of the asparagus. Since asparagus is relatively expensive, indulge yourself and savour this recipe when it is in season. Serve it as a starter or side dish for a special meal.

SERVES 2–4

450 g (1 lb) fresh asparagus

DRESSING

1 teaspoon dried mustard
1 teaspoon hot water
1 egg yolk
1 tablespoon dark soy sauce

1 teaspoon finely chopped fresh
    ginger
¼ teaspoon salt

Break off the woody ends of the asparagus and cut the stalks into 7.5 cm (3 in) diagonal pieces. Blanch the asparagus in a wok or pan of boiling salted water for 2 minutes. Plunge them into cold water, then drain in a colander. Pat dry with kitchen paper.

In a small bowl, mix the mustard and hot water together and stir until a thick paste. Add the rest of the dressing ingredients and mix well.

Arrange the asparagus on a serving platter and pour the dressing over. Serve immediately or within 3 hours.

# CRISPY NOODLE SALAD

*I* first enjoyed this salad, called Mee Krob, in a rather unpretentious restaurant in Bangkok. There are a number of different variations on the crispy noodle salad theme, with many people preferring a sweet and sour salad. At home, I set out to recreate the combination of textures, flavours and colours that had most impressed me in Thailand, and this recipe is my favourite – a beautifully arranged salad platter that is dressed and tossed at the last minute. Such a salad is ideal as a starter for any meal.

SERVES 4

300 ml (10 fl oz) oil (preferably groundnut), for deep-frying
100 g (4 oz) rice noodles, rice vermicelli or rice sticks

Sauce

2 cloves garlic, crushed
2 tablespoons finely chopped shallots
3 tablespoons fish sauce
1 tablespoon sugar
2 tablespoons Chinese white vinegar or cider vinegar

GARNISH

100 g (4 oz) beancurd, cut into small dice
100 g (4 oz) bean sprouts
3 spring onions, shredded
1 fresh chilli, shredded
fresh coriander sprigs

Heat the oil in a wok or deep-fat fryer until moderately hot. Deep-fry the noodles until crispy and puffed up. Remove from the oil with a slotted spoon and drain on kitchen paper. You may have to do this in several batches. (Leave the oil in the wok or deep-fat fryer as you will need it for the beancurd.)

Cut the beancurd into 1 cm (½ in) cubes. Reheat the oil until very hot and deep-fry the beancurd cubes until golden. Remove with a slotted spoon and drain on kitchen paper.

Combine the sauce ingredients in a small bowl and mix well.

Place the crispy noodles on a serving platter and garnish attractively with the beancurd, bean sprouts, spring onions, chilli and coriander. Pour the dressing over the salad just before serving and mix well.

# VEGETABLE DISHES

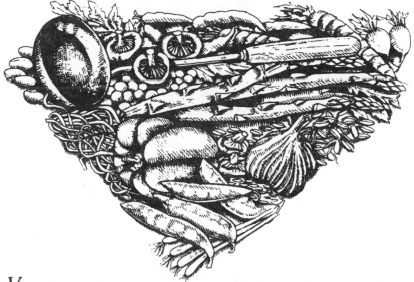

*V*egetables are important in any cuisine that is nutritious, flavourful and colourful. In the Cantonese cuisine of south China, considered among the most nutritious in the world, more vegetables of diverse texture, shape, size and colour are used than in almost any other culinary tradition.

Many vegetables have delicate textures; most have only subtle flavours. How does one cook them and yet preserve their qualities? Well, practice makes perfect, especially to avoid overcooking. With vegetables, you need to nibble, taste, nibble, taste as you cook.

If vegetables in the raw state are soft, leafy, delicate and full of moisture, like spinach, Chinese greens and lettuce, they need very little cooking. A simple blanching or quick stir-frying in a little oil with intense heat will cook them to perfection.

Some vegetables such as courgettes, mangetout, peppers and cucumbers need to be cooked a little longer than you would the more tender, leafy ones. 'Salting' is usually a good technique for preparing courgettes and cucumbers for cooking. This methods draws out some of the liquid while preserving their textures and flavours.

'Hard' vegetables, such as carrots, broccoli, cauliflower and Brussels sprouts usually require two separate cooking procedures – blanching to soften them and then stir-frying to cook them sufficiently and infuse them with additional flavours. Aubergines, bitter melon and Chinese leaves profit from more extensive cooking. Some release additional liquid or bitter juices in the cooking process.

If you are cooking a multi-vegetable dish or combining vegetables with other foods such as meat, fish or poultry, you can cook the different vegetables separately and *then* combine everything at the last moment. The result will be perfectly cooked because every element of the dish will have had its own correct cooking time.

Finally, a great deal of vegetable cookery involves common sense and experience. Don't worry, and trust your own judgement. If you made a mistake, it will be a valuable lesson for your next attempt.

# BUTTON MUSHROOMS IN OYSTER SAUCE

*B*utton mushrooms are unknown in the East, but I have found that they, like all good edible fungi, are perfectly amenable to Chinese and other Southeast Asian spices and seasoning. Here I have combined them with the classic southern Chinese flavour of oyster sauce.

SERVES 2–4

2 teaspoons oil (preferably groundnut)
2 garlic cloves, crushed
450 g (1 lb) small whole button mushrooms

1 tablespoon dark soy sauce
1 tablespoon oyster sauce
1 teaspoon sugar
2 tablespoons rice wine or dry sherry

Heat a wok or large frying-pan and add the oil. Put in the garlic and stir-fry for 30 seconds. Add the mushrooms and stir-fry for 1 minute. Stir in the soy sauce, oyster sauce, sugar and rice wine. Turn the heat down and simmer slowly for 5 minutes, stirring from time to time. When the mushrooms are cooked, turn the heat back to high and continue stirring until most of the liquid has evaporated and the dish is ready to be served.

# SUMMER PEPPER STIR-FRY

*H*ere is an ensemble of colours, flavours, tastes and textures that will appeal to the eye as well as the palate.

SERVES 2–4

25 g (1 oz) Chinese dried mushrooms

2 eggs, beaten

1 teaspoon sesame oil

¼ teaspoon salt

5 teaspoons oil (preferably groundnut)

1 tablespoon finely chopped spring onions

1 tablespoon finely chopped fresh ginger

1 tablespoon finely chopped garlic

1 small fresh chilli, seeded and finely shredded

225 g (8 oz) red, yellow or green peppers (about 1 each)

2 teaspoons rice wine or dry sherry

1 teaspoon light soy sauce

1 teaspoon sugar

salt and freshly ground black pepper to taste

100 g (4 oz) bean sprouts, preferably trimmed at both ends

2 teaspoons sesame oil

GARNISH

2 tablespoons finely chopped spring onions

Soak the dried mushrooms in warm water for 20 minutes or until soft. Squeeze out the excess water and cut away the stalks. Shred the mushroom caps and set aside.

Combine the beaten eggs with the 1 teaspoon of sesame oil and salt in a small bowl. Heat a work or frying-pan over moderate heat and add 2 teaspoons of the groundnut oil. Add the egg mixture and spread over the surface of the pan until it forms a thin crêpe-like pancake. Remove from the heat and, when cool, cut the egg pancake into thin shreds and set aside.

Heat a wok or large frying-pan over high heat and add the remaining groundnut oil. Put in the spring onions, ginger, garlic and chilli and stir-fry for 30 seconds. Add the peppers, mushrooms, rice wine, soy sauce, sugar, salt and pepper. Stir-fry for 2 minutes until the peppers are soft. Stir in the bean sprouts and egg shreds and stir-fry gently for another 2 minutes, then add the 2 teaspoons of sesame oil. Remove the mixture to a serving platter and garnish with the spring onions. Serve at once.

# RAINBOW VEGETABLES IN LETTUCE CUPS

*I*n this version of a popular Hong Kong dish, one that usually includes minced lean beef, pigeon or pork, I use only vegetables. The meat or poultry are not missed when one savours the tasty crunchiness of the vegetables combined with crispy fried bean thread noodles, cupped in a refreshing lettuce leaf and flavoured with hoisin sauce. This dish makes a good starter for a festive meal, as guests can fill their own lettuce cups at the table.

SERVES 4

350 g (12 oz) iceberg lettuce
100 g (4 oz) carrots
225 g (8 oz) courgettes
100 g (4 oz) red peppers
100 g (4 oz) yellow peppers
300 ml (10 fl oz) oil (preferably groundnut), for deep-frying
25 g (1 oz) bean thread (transparent) noodles
3 tablespoons coarsely chopped garlic

½ teaspoon salt
2 tablespoons rice wine or dry sherry
3 tablespoons chicken or vegetable stock
100 g (4 oz) fresh or tinned waterchestnuts, coarsely chopped
2 teaspoons light soy sauce
1½ tablespoons oyster sauce
3 tablespoons hoisin sauce

Separate, wash and dry the lettuce leaves. Finely dice the carrots, courgettes and peppers.

In a deep-fat fryer or large wok, heat the 300 ml (10 fl oz) of oil until almost smoking. Turn off the heat and deep-fry the noodles in batches until they are crisp and puffed up. Drain on kitchen paper.

Heat a wok or large frying-pan and add 1 tablespoon of the oil in which you have fried the noodles. Put in the garlic, salt, carrots, rice wine and stock and stir-fry for about 2 minutes. Then add the rest of the vegetables and waterchestnuts (except the lettuce) together with the soy sauce and stir-fry for 3 minutes. Stir in the oyster sauce and continue to stir-fry for a further minute. Turn the mixture onto a platter. Arrange the lettuce and noodles on separate platters, put the hoisin sauce in a small bowl, and serve.

# STIR-FRIED 'SILVER SPROUTS'

$S$mall mung beans provide these sprouts. They are a very nutritious addition to salads and stir-fried dishes, their mild flavour and crunchiness providing a delightful touch to every meal. When they are stir-fried with beancurd and other ingredients, as here, their colour appears as a shimmering silver, hence the name.

Try to obtain pressed seasoned beancurd. It is cooked in a soy-flavoured sauce which also imparts a pleasant brownish colour to it. If unavailable, you may substitute fresh firm beancurd, but you must weight it down with a heavy lid for at least 2 hours to make it even firmer and less moist. It will also have less flavour, so remember to increase your seasonings. Pan-fry the beancurd until it is firm before stir-frying.

SERVES 4

25 g (1 oz) Chinese dried
  mushrooms
225 g (8 oz) bean sprouts
225 g (8 oz) pressed seasoned
  beancurd or beancurd
50 g (2 oz) celery
100 g (4 oz) green peppers
50 g (2 oz) carrots
4 spring onions

1 tablespoon oil (preferably
  groundnut)
2 teaspoons chilli oil
1½ teaspoons salt
¼ teaspoon freshly ground
  black pepper
2 tablespoons rice wine or dry
  sherry
3–4 tablespoons water

Soak the mushrooms in a large bowl of water for 20 minutes. Drain them and squeeze out any excess liquid. Discard the tough stalks, finely shred the caps and put them aside.

Trim the bean sprouts. Cut the pressed beancurd, celery, peppers, carrots and spring onions into fine shreds.

Heat a wok or large frying-pan over moderate heat and add the oils. Put in the salt, pepper and carrots and stir-fry for 1 minute. Add the celery, mushrooms, beancurd, peppers and spring onions and continue to stir-fry for 2 minutes. Stir in the rice wine and water and stir-fry until most of the liquid has evaporated. Turn onto a plate and serve at once.

# DRY-BRAISED BAMBOO SHOOTS WITH BROCCOLI

*F*resh bamboo shoots are rare outside the Southeast Asian sub-tropics, where they feature in many recipes as a vegetable, as part of a stuffing or as a garnish for meat, seafood and vegetarian dishes. Those of us outside Southeast Asia must make do with the tinned variety. Served with rice, this recipe makes a light and very appetising vegetarian meal.

SERVES 4

| | |
|---|---|
| 225 g (8 oz) fresh broccoli | 1 tablespoon sugar |
| 540 g (1¼ lb) tinned bamboo shoots | 3 tablespoons rice wine or dry sherry |
| 150 ml (5 fl oz) oil (preferably groundnut) | 150 ml (5 fl oz) chicken or vegetable stock |
| 1 teaspoon finely chopped fresh ginger | 1 tablespoon oil (preferably groundnut) |
| 1 teaspoon salt | 2 teaspoons finely chopped garlic |
| 1 tablespoon yellow bean sauce | |

Separate the broccoli heads into florets, then peel the stalks if necessary and slice. Blanch the broccoli pieces in a large pan of boiling, salted water for several minutes. Drain and immerse them in cold water. Drain again thoroughly in a colander and set aside. Rinse the tinned bamboo shoots well.

Cut the bamboo shoots into 7.5 × 1 cm (3 × ½ in) pieces and dry thoroughly with kitchen paper. Heat the 150 ml (5 fl oz) of oil in a wok or large frying-pan. Pan-fry the bamboo shoots until they are nicely brown. Drain thoroughly on kitchen paper and set aside.

Pour off all but 1 teaspoon of the oil and reheat the wok. Add the ginger, ½ teaspoon of the salt and the bean sauce, and stir-fry for 1 minute. Return the bamboo shoots to the wok and add the sugar, rice wine and stock. Braise for 3–5 minutes over high heat until most of the liquid has evaporated. Remove and set aside.

Wipe the wok clean, reheat and add the 1 tablespoon of fresh oil. When smoking slightly, add the garlic, remaining salt and broccoli to the wok and stir-fry for 1 minute. Return the bamboo shoots to the wok and continue to stir-fry for another 2–3 minutes or until heated through. Turn the mixture onto a platter and serve at once.

# MOCK VEGETABLE PASTA

*I*n Chinese vegetarian cookery, a dish is not always what it appears to be. For example, 'mock duck' is taro root stuffed with minced vegetables and fried to a golden brown to look like duck. I enjoy the fun and imaginativeness of such creativity and here I take courgettes and cut them into long thin strips to look like pasta. I then salt them to remove excess moisture and, in the process, firm their texture. Quickly stir-fried with traditional Chinese seasonings, the resulting dish looks and tastes like pasta – my guests are always surprised by its lightness, flavour and texture. Do not overcook the courgettes – you want an *al dente* firmness to the bite. This mock pasta is delicious cold, and it can also function as a vegetable or salad serving; it is perfect for picnics too.

SERVES 4

| | |
|---|---|
| 900 g (2 lb) courgettes | 2 teaspoons finely chopped |
| 1 tablespoon salt | fresh ginger |
| 1 tablespoon oil (preferably | 2 tablespoons finely chopped |
| groundnut) | fresh coriander |
| 1 tablespoon finely chopped | 2 tablespooons finely chopped |
| garlic | spring onions, green parts only |

Cut the courgettes into long thin strips resembling pasta. Put the strips into a colander and sprinkle with the salt. Leave to stand for 20 minutes. Then wrap the courgettes in a linen tea towel and squeeze out the excess liquid.

Heat a wok or large frying-pan over moderate heat and add the oil. Put in the garlic and ginger and stir-fry for 30 seconds. Add the courgettes, fresh coriander and spring onions and continue to stir-fry for 4 minutes or until the courgettes are heated through. Turn the mixture onto a platter and serve warm or at room temperature.

# Asparagus with Chinese Black Mushrooms

Asparagus is a vegetable which readily combines with many other foods in the most congenial fashion. Here, it is joined with meaty, smokey Chinese dried mushrooms, with both vegetables absorbing the essences of each other and of the sauce. I suggest that, if available, you use a larger variety of asparagus. This is a wholesome and satisfying dish, easy to prepare and, with rice, a meal in itself.

SERVES 2–4

| | |
|---|---|
| 450 g (1 lb) large asparagus | ¼ teaspoon salt |
| 25 g (1 oz) Chinese dried mushrooms | 150 ml (5 fl oz) chicken or vegetable stock |
| 1 tablespoon oil (preferably groundnut) | 2 tablespoons oyster sauce |
| 2 cloves garlic, lightly crushed | 1 teaspoon cornflour mixed with 1 teaspoon cold water |

Cut the asparagus diagonally into 5 cm (2 in) lengths, discarding the hard woody ends.

Soak the dried mushrooms in warm water for about 20 minutes. Remove the mushrooms from the water and squeeze out any excess liquid. Cut off the stalks and discard them.

Heat a wok or large frying-pan over moderate heat and add the oil. Put in the garlic, salt and asparagus and stir-fry for 1 minute. Add the stock and mushrooms and continue to stir-fry for 3 minutes or until the asparagus is cooked. Add the oyster sauce and blended cornflour and continue to cook until the sauce has been reduced to a glaze. Give the mixture a final stir, turn into a platter and serve at once.

# GREEN BEANS IN
# PUNGENT SAUCE

*I* often enjoyed this easy-to-make homely dish as a child. Fresh green beans are a nutritious and inexpensive vegetable and lend themselves to spices and seasonings that complement their delicate flavour. In this recipe, the pungent spiciness of fermented chilli beancurd turns the vegetable into something quite special. You will find fermented beancurd at Chinese grocers: you may choose from various types, ranging from mild to quite spicy. In using so lively a spice as chilli beancurd, remember that a little goes a long way.

SERVES 2–4

1 tablespoon oil (preferably groundnut)

2 garlic cloves, crushed

1 tablespoon fermented chilli beancurd or chilli sauce

¼ teaspoon salt

450 g (1 lb) runner beans, trimmed and sliced, or French beans, trimmed and left whole

3 tablespoons rice wine or dry sherry

2 tablespoons water

Heat a wok or large frying-pan and add the oil. When moderately hot, add the garlic, beancurd and salt and stir-fry for about 30 seconds. Add the beans, rice wine and water and continue to stir-fry over a moderately high heat for about 5 minutes or until the beans are thoroughly cooked, adding more water if necessary to keep the beans moist. Serve at once.

# SICHUAN FRIED AUBERGINES

*A*ubergines are delicious when fried in a light batter, which prevents too much oil penetrating the aubergines. They are then enlivened by what the Chinese call a 'fish flavouring' sauce, a non-fishy mixture of spices and seasonings normally used in the preparation of fish. Both the aubergines and the batter readily absorb the sauce. This sauce is not to be confused with the commercially bottled fish sauce widely used in Southeast Asian cooking. Try to buy Chinese aubergines as they have a more delicate taste; however, ordinary aubergines will suffice.

SERVES 4

350 g (12 oz) aubergines
450 ml (15 fl oz) oil (preferably groundnut), for deep-frying

Sauce
1 tablespoon oil (preferably groundnut)
3 tablespoons finely chopped spring onions
1 tablespoon finely chopped fresh ginger
2 teaspoons chilli bean sauce
150 ml (5 fl oz) chicken or vegetable stock

Batter
50 g (2 oz) plain flour
150 ml (5 fl oz) water
¼ teaspoon salt

2 tablespoons rice wine or dry sherry
1 tablespoon Chinese black rice vinegar or cider vinegar
3 tablespoons tomato purée
2 teaspoons sugar
2 tablespoons dark soy sauce
1 teaspoon cornflour mixed with 1 teaspoon water

Cut the aubergines into 3.5 × 7.5 cm (1½ × 3 in) slices. Do not peel them. For the batter, mix the flour, water and salt together in a small bowl, then strain through a fine sieve. Leave to rest for about 20 minutes.

For the sauce, heat a wok or large frying-pan until hot and add the 1 tablespoon oil. Put in the spring onions, ginger and chilli bean sauce and stir-fry for 30 seconds. Then add the stock, rice wine, vinegar, tomato purée, sugar and soy sauce and continue to cook for 1 minute. Thicken the sauce with the blended cornflour and cook for another minute. Set aside.

Heat the oil in a deep-fat fryer or large wok until quite hot. Dip the slices of aubergine into the batter, let the excess batter drip off, then deep-fry. You may have to do this in several batches. Remove from the oil with a slotted spoon and drain well on kitchen paper. Arrange the aubergine slices on a serving platter, pour the sauce over and serve.

# STIR-FRIED LETTUCE

*L*ettuce is used so often in the West as a garnish and salad that one tends to forget it is a vegetable and, as such, capable of a greater culinary role. As a child at home, I ate only cooked lettuce and I was a bit put off to see my Western friends eating it raw in their lunch sandwiches. In Hong Kong, the street-side food vendors or food stalls offer stir-fried lettuce as a vegetable dish to accompany rice and chicken dishes. It works very well, provided you use firm lettuce and stir-fry it very quickly.

SERVES 2–4

450 g (1 lb) iceberg or cos lettuce

1 tablespoon oil (preferably groundnut)

2 garlic cloves, crushed

1 teaspoon finely chopped fresh ginger

3 tablespoons chicken or vegetable stock

1 tablespoon light soy sauce

¼ teaspoon salt

1 teaspoon sugar

½ teaspoon cornflour mixed with 1 teaspoon water

Separate the lettuce leaves and wash well. Cut the large leaves in half.

Heat a wok or large frying-pan and add the oil. When moderately hot, add the garlic and ginger and stir-fry for 30 seconds. Next add the lettuce and stir-fry quickly for a few seconds. Stir in the rest of the ingredients, except the cornflour mixture. Give a couple of stirs and then remove the lettuce to a platter with a slotted spoon. Add the blended cornflour to the sauce and bring to the boil. When the sauce thickens, pour over the lettuce and serve at once.

# STIR-FRIED CUCUMBERS

Cucumbers are too often taken for granted, their cool unobtrusive virtues having rendered them less interesting than other vegetables and fit only for salad. Stir-fried, however, they take on an unexpected boldness. My uncle used to cook them with little pieces of pork, but I have learned that they are tasty all by themselves with a complementary sauce. Salt the cucumbers first to rid them of their excess liquid. Stir-fried and made savoury by the sauce, the cucumbers make a wonderful vegetable side dish that is ideal for lunch or dinner.

SERVES 4

750 g (1½ lb) cucumbers
(about 2 small)
2¼ teaspoons salt
1 tablespoon oil (preferably groundnut)

2 tablespoons dark soy sauce
1 tablespoon rice wine or dry sherry
2 teaspoons sesame oil
1 teaspoon chilli oil

Peel the cucumbers, slice them in half lengthways and, using a teaspoon, remove the seeds. Cut the cucumber halves into 7.5 cm (3 in) lengths. Sprinkle them with 2 teaspoons of the salt and mix well. Put the salted cucumbers into a colander and leave for 20 minutes to drain. This rids the cucumbers of any excess liquid. When the cucumber pieces have drained, rinse in water and then blot dry with kitchen paper.

Heat a wok or large frying-pan until hot and add the oil. Put in the cucumber and stir-fry for 2 minutes. Stir in the remaining salt, soy sauce and rice wine and continue to stir-fry for another 2 minutes. Add the sesame and chilli oils and give the mixture several good stirs. Serve at once.

# STIR-FRIED SPICY CARROTS

The European carrot is now the standard in China and in Chinese cookery, although the Chinese do cultivate a larger version which is also quite sweet. Because of their distinctive taste and colour, carrots combine well with other seasonings and herbs, in this case the pungent flavours of ginger, black beans, garlic and dried chillies. These colourful and tasty carrots go well with a simple serving of plain rice or as a pleasing vegetable dish accompanying meat or poultry. They can also be served at room temperature, making them an interesting addition to any picnic menu.

SERVES 4

750 g (1½ lb) carrots
1 tablespoon oil (preferably groundnut)
2 teaspoons finely chopped garlic
1 teaspoon finely chopped fresh ginger

2 dried chillies, seeded
1 tablespoon black beans, coarsely chopped
1 teaspoon sugar
2 tablespoons rice wine or dry sherry
2 teaspoons sesame oil

Peel the carrots and cut diagonally into chunks. Blanch the carrots in a large pan of boiling salted water for 4–5 minutes, then immerse them in cold water. Drain thoroughly.

Heat a wok or large frying-pan until moderately hot and add the oil. Put in the garlic, ginger, chillies and black beans and stir-fry for about 1 minute. Stir in the carrots, sugar and rice wine and continue to stir-fry for about 3 minutes or until the carrots are thoroughly heated. Add the sesame oil and continue to stir-fry for 20 seconds.

# CRISPY VEGETABLE STIR-FRY

*I* like to serve meals that appeal to the eye as well as to the palate. There-fore, when peppers are in season I use them as often as possible: the sweetness of the reds and yellows and the mild bite of the greens delight one's senses and add a colourful dimension to any meal. Stir-frying pre-serves the best characteristics of peppers. When combined, as here, with the crisp texture and sweet flavour of bamboo shoots and waterchestnuts and the zing of ginger, the result is a colourful and healthy vegetable dish. Use fresh waterchestnuts if possible.

Remember that the key to stir-frying vegetables is to cook the harder ones, or those with the least amount of moisture, first.

SERVES 4

100 g (4 oz) red peppers
100 g (4 oz) green peppers
100 g (4 oz) yellow peppers
100 g (4 oz) fresh or tinned
    (drained weight)
    waterchestnuts
50 g (2 oz) tinned (drained
    weight) bamboo shoots

2 teaspoons oil (preferably
    groundnut)
2 teaspoons salt
3 slices fresh ginger
50 g (2 oz) mangetout, trimmed
3 tablespoons water

Cut the peppers into 3.5 cm (1½ in) triangles. Thinly slice the waterchestnuts and bamboo shoots.

Heat a wok or large frying-pan and add the oil. When moderately hot, add the salt and ginger and stir-fry for about 1 minute to allow the ginger to flavour the oil. Add the peppers and stir-fry for 2 minutes. Stir in the waterchestnuts and bamboo shoots and continue to stir-fry for 2 minutes. Finally add the mangetout and stir-fry for 30 seconds, then add the water. Stir-fry for another minute or until the mangetout are cooked, adding more water if necessary. When the vegetables are cooked, serve them at once.

# HOME-STYLE SPICY BEANCURD

*T*his recipe is my adaptation of 'Ma Po's home-cooked beancurd', a popular and traditional Sichuan dish I first experienced in a Sichuan-style restaurant in Hong Kong. The Sichuan style emphasises hot spices and strong seasonings, with which beancurd readily combines. I have made this into a vegetarian dish by omitting the minced beef or pork that is normally used. Beancurd is such a good protein and the sauce and garnish are so full of flavour that the meat is not missed, either nutritionally or as a taste. Note that here I use *soft* beancurd, so that the result is a spicy and savoury custard-like dish, perfect with rice, crispy noodles or bread.

SERVES 2–4

450 g (1 lb) soft beancurd, drained

1 tablespoon oil (preferably groundnut)

1 tablespoon finely chopped fresh ginger

1 tablespoon finely chopped garlic

1 tablespoon chilli bean sauce

1 teaspoon yellow bean sauce

2 teaspoons sugar

50 ml (2 fl oz) chicken or vegetable stock

2 tablespoons rice wine or dry sherry

1 teaspoon cornflour mixed with 1 teaspoon water

GARNISH

2 teaspoons sesame oil

2 tablespoons finely chopped spring onions

Cut the beancurd into 2.5 cm (1 in) cubes and set aside. Heat a wok or large frying-pan over high heat and add the oil. Put in the ginger, garlic, chilli bean sauce and yellow bean sauce and stir-fry for 30 seconds. Add the sugar, stock and rice wine and cook for 2 minutes. Stir the blended cornflour into the wok. When the sauce has slightly thickened, add the beancurd cubes and stir gently. Continue to cook for 2 minutes or until the beancurd is heated through. Garnish and serve at once.

# SWEET AND SOUR BEANCURD

Sweet and sour sauces must never be too sweet or too vinegary. When properly made they are a delight. As the contrasting tastes alternate and combine in the palate, one understands why well-prepared sweet and sour dishes are justly praised classics. Such a sauce lends itself to many different types of food but combines particularly well with beancurd.

SERVES 2–4

450 g (1 lb) firm beancurd
300 ml (10 fl oz) oil (preferably groundnut), for deep-frying
50 g (2 oz) carrots
50 g (2 oz) red pepper
450 g (1 lb) fresh pineapple or 275 g (10 oz) tinned pineapple

Sauce
2 garlic cloves, crushed
2 tablespoons tomato purée
1 tablespoon white rice vinegar or cider vinegar
2 tablespoons rice wine or dry sherry
1 tablespoon light soy sauce
1 tablespoon sugar
150 ml (5 fl oz) chicken or vegetable stock
2 teaspoons cornflour mixed with 2 teaspoons water

GARNISH

fresh coriander leaves

Cut the beancurd into 2.5 cm (1 in) cubes. Heat the oil in a deep-fat fryer or large wok. When the oil is almost smoking, deep-fry the beancurd cubes. You may have to do this in several batches. Drain on kitchen paper and set aside.

Cut the carrots into 2.5 cm (1 in) rounds and blanch in a small pan of boiling water for 3 minutes. Drain and set aside. Cut the pepper into 2.5 cm (1 in) squares. Peel, core and cut the pineapple into 2.5 cm (1 in) cubes.

Combine the sauce ingredients, except the cornflour, together in a wok or pan and bring to the boil. Add the carrot and red pepper and stir well. Stir the blended cornflour into the sauce and bring it back to the boil. Reduce the heat to simmering point and gently put in the beancurd and pineapple. Mix well, then turn the mixture onto a deep platter. Garnish and serve at once.

# PASTA AND NOODLES

$P$asta or noodles come in many forms in China, Japan and Southeast Asia. These are made from wheat, rice, buck-wheat, bean threads or yam threads. Throughout these areas, pasta is eaten in the form of noodles, wuntuns and pasta wrappers. These foods have been a part of the diet of this region for many hundreds of years.

All pasta is characterised by subtle variations of texture and colour, absorbent receptivity to sauces and congeniality to other foods, plus excellent nutritional values. Its universal popularity is therefore not surprising.

The word 'pasta' is, of course, an Italian word. I use it because it has entered our language as a generic term meaning unleavened dough, rolled out and formed into different shapes. One regional difference is that some oriental pastas are made from rice flour rather than wheat.

# SPICY BEAN THREAD NOODLES
# WITH DRIED SHRIMPS

*T*hese noodles have a smooth, light texture that readily absorbs the surrounding flavours. In this recipe I follow my mother's example. Because most of the work involved can be done the day before and because the dish reheats so well, this may be called gourmet fast food. After a hard day's work, my mother preferred to serve a meal that was easily prepared yet full of flavour, and this was one of her favourites. Take care when cooking the noodles because if they overcook they tend to lump together. Although the bean thread are known as noodles, this dish is delicious served with rice also.

SERVES 2–4

25 g (1 oz) Chinese dried
  mushrooms
175 g (6 oz) bean thread
  (transparent) noodles
2 tablespoons oil (preferably
  groundnut)
2 tablespoons finely chopped
  garlic
1 tablespoon finely chopped
  fresh ginger

2 tablespoons finely chopped
  shallots
2 teaspoons chilli bean sauce
2 teaspoons light soy sauce
2 teaspoons sugar
2 tablespoons rice wine or dry
  sherry
2 teaspoons chilli oil

GARNISH

3 tablespoons finely chopped spring onions, green part only

Soak the dried mushrooms in warm water for 20 minutes. Drain them, squeeze out any excess liquid, cut off and discard the stalks and coarsely chop the mushrooms caps. Soak the noodles in a large bowl of warm water for 15 minutes. When soft, drain the noodles well. Cut into 7.5 cm (3 in) lengths, using scissors or a knife.

Heat a wok or pan and add the oil. Put in the garlic, ginger, shallot and chilli bean sauce and stir-fry quickly for a few seconds. Add the mushrooms and noodles and stir-fry for about 2 minutes. Stir in the soy sauce, sugar, rice wine and chilli oil and continue to cook the mixture over a gentle heat for about 5 minutes. Ladle the noodles into a large serving bowl, garnish with the spring onions and serve at once.

# SPINACH AND RICE NOODLES

*I*n this quick and healthy light meal, the dried noodles need only to be soaked and require very little cooking. Their texture is such that the spinach flavour, some of the colour and other seasonings are readily absorbed. Unlike egg noodles, rice noodles do not become sticky and gummy when they are moist; this makes it convenient to serve them cold. I add a little sugar to neutralise the iron and salt taste of the spinach.

SERVES 2–4

750 g (1½ lb) fresh spinach
100 g (4 oz) rice noodles, rice vermicelli or rice sticks
1 tablespoon oil (preferably groundnut)
1 teaspoon salt

2 tablespoons coarsely chopped garlic
2 teaspoons sugar
1 tablespoon light soy sauce
2 teaspoons chilli oil

Wash the spinach thoroughly. Remove all the stalks, leaving just the leaves.

Soak the rice noodles in a bowl of warm water for 25 minutes. Then drain them in a colander or sieve. (If you are using dried egg noodles, cook them for 3–5 minutes in boiling water, drain and immerse in cold water until required.)

Heat a wok or large pan to moderate heat and add the oil. Put in the salt and garlic and stir-fry for a few seconds. Add the spinach leaves and stir-fry for 2 minutes to coat the spinach leaves thoroughly. When the spinach has wilted to about a third of its original size, add the rice noodles, sugar, soy sauce and chilli oil, and continue to stir-fry for another 4 minutes. Transfer the noodles to a plate, and pour off any excess liquid. Serve hot or cold.

# KOREAN BEAN THREAD SESAME NOODLES WITH VEGETABLES

*B*ean thread noodles are made from the starch of the mung bean and, when cooked, they are almost transparent. This simple to prepare recipe is my version of a popular Korean dish. What makes it memorable is the combination of lace-like noodles and exotic mushrooms, and unusual mixture of tastes and textures.

SERVES 4

25 g (1 oz) Chinese dried
mushrooms
15 g (½ oz) Chinese dried
cloud ears (black fungus)
100 g (4 oz) bean thread
(transparent) noodles
2 tablespoons oil (preferably
groundnut)
50 g (2 oz) carrot, shredded
1 small onion, shredded
1 green pepper, shredded
120 ml (4 fl oz) water

Sauce
2 tablespoons light soy sauce
2 tablespoons dark soy sauce
3 tablespoons sesame oil
1½ tablespoons sesame seeds
1 tablespoon finely chopped
garlic
1 tablespoon sugar
1 teaspoon freshly ground black
pepper

Soak the dried mushrooms in warm water for 20 minutes until soft. Squeeze the excess liquid from the mushrooms and remove and discard the stalks. Cut the caps into shreds. Soak the cloud ears in warm water for about 20 minutes or until soft. Rinse them well in cold water and drain thoroughly in a colander.

Soak the noodles in a large bowl of very hot water for 15 minutes. When soft, drain well. Cut the noodles into 7.5 cm (3 in) lengths, using scissors or a knife.

Heat a wok or large frying-pan and add the oil. When moderately hot, add the mushrooms, cloud ears, carrot, onion, green pepper and water and stir-fry for 5 minutes or until the carrots are cooked.

Combine the sauce ingredients and add them to the vegetables. Give the mixture a good stir, then add the noodles. Stir-fry the mixture for 2 minutes until well heated through. Serve at once or at room temperature.

# TAN TAN NOODLES

To warm up on a cold afternoon or evening, serve Tan Tan noodles, which I first tasted in a Sichuan restaurant in Hong Kong. Given its Sichuan origin, I expected something spicy – but even so, I was quite unprepared for its explosive quality. The noodles arrived preceded by a wonderful aroma and were served in a bowl shimmering with red chilli oil. It was a delightful experience, featuring the classical spiciness of chilli beans, garlic and ginger. I immediately tried to recreate the noodles when I returned home. The result is this recipe and I have enjoyed the noodles many times since. If you can find the Sichuan preserved vegetable in an oriental store, it will give a truly authentic taste.

SERVES 2

1 tablespoon oil (preferably groundnut)

100 g (4 oz) Sichuan preserved cabbage or vegetable, rinsed and finely chopped (optional)

1 tablespoon finely chopped garlic

2 teaspoons finely chopped fresh ginger

2 tablespoons rice wine or dry sherry

1 tablespoon chilli bean sauce

1 tablespoon Chinese sesame paste or peanut butter

1 tablespoon dark soy sauce

1 tablespoon sugar

450 ml (15 fl oz) chicken or vegetable stock

225 g (8 oz) Chinese fresh or dried flat thin wheat or egg noodles

Heat a wok or large frying-pan over high heat and add the oil. Put in the preserved cabbage or vegetable if using, the garlic and ginger and stir-fry for 1 minute. Add the rice wine, chilli bean sauce, sesame paste, soy sauce, sugar and stock. Reduce the heat and simmer for 3 minutes over low heat.

Bring a large pan of water to the boil and cook the noodles for 2 minutes if they are fresh and 5 minutes if dried. Drain well in a colander. Divide the noodles into individual bowls and ladle the sauce over them. Serve at once.

# CRISPY CANTONESE-STYLE NOODLES WITH VEGETABLES

*T*he origins of pasta are obscured by time and controversy, but there is a general consensus that the Chinese first thought of the egg noodle variety. Whoever invented the process, pan-fried noodles make a perfect foundation for stir-fired dishes.

SERVES 2–4

25 g (1 oz) button mushrooms
6 spring onions
100 g (4 oz) red pepper
50 g (2 oz) celery
225 g (8 oz) dried or fresh thin
   Chinese egg noodles
2 tablespoons oil (preferably
   groundnut)
4 garlic cloves, lightly crushed
100 g (4 oz) mangetout, trimmed

2 teaspoons light soy sauce
2 tablespoons oyster sauce
2 teaspoons sugar
3 tablespoons rice wine or dry
   sherry
300 ml (10 fl oz) chicken or
   vegetable stock
2 teaspoons cornflour mixed
   with 2 teaspoons water

Finely shred the mushrooms, spring onions and pepper. Coarsely chop the celery.

If you are using dried noodles, cook them according to the instructions on the packet, otherwise boil for 2 minutes until soft. If you are using fresh Chinese noodles, boil for 3 minutes then drain thoroughly.

Heat a large frying-pan, preferably non-stick, and add 1 tablespoon of the oil. When hot, add the noodles and press down to make the noodles conform to the shape of the pan. Turn the heat to very low, and continue cooking for 10–15 minutes, until brown. Flip the noodles over in one piece and continue cooking them until the other side is brown.

While the noodles are browning, heat a wok or large frying-pan until hot. Add the remaining oil and garlic and stir-fry for a few seconds. Put in the celery, mushrooms and pepper and stir-fry for 3 minutes. Add the mangetout and spring onions and continue to stir-fry for another 2 minutes. Stir in the soy sauce, oyster sauce, sugar, rice wine and stock, and bring to the boil. Thicken with blended cornflour. Take out the noodles and place on a platter. Pour the sauce and vegetables over the noodles and serve.

# HOT AND SOUR NOODLES

*H*ot and sour is a popular combination in Chinese cookery. We Chinese love the two compatible tastes on our palate. This type of noodle dish is often served in snack noodle shops or food stalls in China and Hong Kong. It serves as a quick fast-food meal that is full of flavour and easily made. I prefer to eat it hot, but it is also good cold. This makes a speedy lunch dish.

SERVES 2–4

450 g (1 lb) fresh or dried egg
   noodles
1 tablespoon sesame oil

Sauce
2 tablespoons dark soy sauce
1 tablespoon chilli oil
1 tablespoon Chinese black rice
   vinegar or cider vinegar
3 tablespoons finely chopped
   spring onions
¼ teaspoon freshly ground
   black pepper
1 teaspoon sugar

If you are using fresh noodles, cook first by boiling them for 3–5 minutes in a large pan of boiling water. If you are using dried noodles, cook in boiling water for 4–5 minutes. Drain the noodles, toss them in the sesame oil and then put aside until required.

Heat all the sauce ingredients in a small pan. Turn the heat down to low and simmer for 5 minutes.

Plunge the noodles into boiling water for 20 seconds, then drain them well in a colander or sieve. Quickly tip the noodles into a large bowl and pour the hot sauce over the top. Mix everything together well and serve at once.

# SINGAPORE-STYLE RICE NOODLES

Rice noodles are lighter than wheat noodles and therefore lend themselves to dishes that are subtle and delicate. Singapore-style rice noodles are just such a treat. Whenever I visit Singapore or Hong Kong I sample this popular favourite, and I am never disappointed. The recipe traditionally includes tiny fresh shrimps and shredded ham and you may add some if you wish, but this recipe is appetising and pleasing vegetarian fare. The thin light noodles blend perfectly with the vegetables and curry sauce. This is equally delicious warm or cold, which makes it perfect for a picnic.

SERVES 2–4

225 g (8 oz) rice noodles, rice vermicelli or rice sticks
100 g (4 oz) leeks
100 g (4 oz) carrots
100 g (4 oz) red peppers
4 spring onions
25 g (1 oz) fresh chillies
2 eggs, beaten
2 teaspoons sesame oil
2 teaspoons salt
2 tablespoons oil (preferably groundnut)

Sauce
2 tablespoons curry paste
1 tablespoon finely chopped garlic
1 tablespoon finely chopped fresh ginger
300 ml (10 fl oz) chicken or vegetable stock
1 tablespoon sugar
2 tablespoons rice wine or dry sherry
2 tablespoons light soy sauce

GARNISH

fresh coriander leaves

Soak the rice noodles in a bowl of warm water for 25 minutes. Drain in a colander or sieve. (If you are using dried egg noodles, cook for 3–5 minutes in boiling water, drain and immerse them in cold water until required.)

Wash and finely shred the white part of the leeks. Finely shred the carrots, peppers, spring onions and chilli. In a small bowl, combine the eggs with the sesame oil and salt.

Heat a wok or large pan over a high heat and add the oil. When almost smoking, add the carrots, leeks and spring onions and stir-fry for a few seconds. Add the peppers and stir-fry for about 1 minute. Put in the curry sauce ingredients and the drained noodles. Stir-fry the mixture for about 5 minutes until well mixed and heated through. Then add the egg mixture, blending thoroughly. Stir-fry for 1 further minute. Serve at once, garnished with fresh coriander.

# LIGHT AND EASY
# RICE NOODLES

*M*aking my way through the streets of Hong Kong and other Asian cities, I have often paused at kerbside food stalls to enjoy this 'fast food' dish. It is light but sustaining and easy to digest as you go about your business. This recipe makes a quick lunch for two using either fresh or dried flat rice noodles.

SERVES 2

225 g (8 oz) dried flat rice
noodles

Sauce
2 tablespoons hoisin sauce
1½ tablespoons light soy sauce
2 teaspoons chilli bean sauce
1 tablespoon sesame oil

GARNISH

1 tablespoon sesame seeds, toasted

If you are using dried rice noodles, bring a large pan of water to the boil, remove it from the heat and add the rice noodles. Leave to stand for about 10 minutes, then drain thoroughly. If you are using fresh rice noodles, set up a steamer or fill a wok or deep casserole with at least 5 cm (2 in) of water. Put a rack into the wok or casserole and bring the water to the boil. Put the rice noodles onto a deep plate and lower the plate into the steamer or onto the rack. Cover the wok tightly. Gently steam on a low heat for 15–20 minutes.

Combine the sauce ingredients and pour over the softened or steamed noodles. Garnish with the sesame seeds and serve.

# VEGETARIAN CHOW MEIN

Chow mein literally means 'stir-fried noodles'. It is a dish of universal popularity based upon its characteristic savoury combination of textures, tastes and colours whether made with meat or, as in this case, with vegetables. Chow mein can be kept warm for at least an hour without losing any of its charm; I enjoy it cold. Serve as an economical family meal or at a buffet party.

SERVES 4

225 g (8 oz) fresh or dried egg noodles
50 g (2 oz) celery
50 g (2 oz) tinned bamboo shoots
2 tablespoons oil (preferably groundnut)
3 garlic cloves, crushed
1 small onion, finely sliced
175 g (6 oz) small button mushrooms

1 tablespoon light soy sauce
2 tablespoons dark soy sauce
2 teaspoons finely chopped fresh ginger
3 tablespoons chicken or vegetable stock
1 tablespoon rice wine or dry sherry
1 teaspoon sugar
100 g (4 oz) bean sprouts

GARNISH

fresh coriander sprigs

If you are using fresh noodles, blanch them first in a large pan of boiling water for 3–5 minutes. If you are using the dried noodles, cook in boiling water for 4–5 minutes. Drain the noodles, then put into cold water until required.

String the celery and slice diagonally. Shred the bamboo shoots.

Heat a wok or large frying-pan and add the oil. When moderately hot, add the garlic and stir-fry for 10 seconds. Add the onion, mushrooms, celery and bamboo shoots and stir-fry for about 5 minutes. Drain the noodles thoroughly and put into the wok. Continue to stir-fry for 1 minute, then add the rest of the ingredients, except the bean sprouts. Continue to stir-fry for another 2 minutes, then stir in the bean sprouts. Give the mixture a good stir and turn in onto a serving platter. Garnish with the fresh coriander sprigs.

# STIR-FRIED VEGETABLES OVER A RICE NOODLE CLOUD

At Chinese banquets when I was a child, the food we children enjoyed most were the dishes that featured fried rice noodles. I believe this is still true today for Western children whose parents take them to Chinese restaurants. Practically any stir-fried dish with a little sauce makes a wonderful topping for these crisp, crackling, crunchy noodles.

SERVES 4

300 ml (10 fl oz) oil (preferably groundnut), for deep-frying
175 g (6 oz) rice noodles, rice vermicelli or rice sticks
225 g (8 oz) aubergines
225 g (8 oz) courgettes
3 garlic cloves, crushed
4 spring onions, chopped
2 tablespoons rice wine or dry sherry
2 tablespoons yellow bean sauce
2 teaspoons chilli bean sauce
150 ml (5 fl oz) chicken or vegetable stock
1 teaspoon sugar
2 tablespoons dark soy sauce
1 teaspoon salt
1 teaspoon cornflour mixed with 1 teaspoon water

Heat the oil in a deep-fat fryer or large wok until very hot. Deep-fry the noodles until they are crisp and puffed up. Remove with a slotted spoon and drain on kitchen paper. You may have to do this in several batches.

Cut the aubergines and courgettes into 7.5 cm (3 in) lengths. Sprinkle them with salt and leave in a sieve to drain for 20 minutes. Rinse under cold running water and pat dry with kitchen paper.

Heat a wok or large frying-pan and add 1½ tablespoons of the oil in which you have fried the noodles. When moderately hot, add the garlic and spring onions and stir-fry for 30 seconds. Add the aubergines and courgettes and continue to stir-fry for 1 minute. Stir in the rest of the ingredients, except for the cornflour mixture, and cook for 3 minutes. Finally add the blended cornflour and cook for a further 1 minute.

Place the deep-fried noodles on a platter and spoon the vegetables over the top. Serve immediately.

# SINGAPORE NOODLES

Singapore is a crossroads city in many ways, including the culinary. This delicious noodle recipe reflects just that, with its combination of Indian, Thai and Chinese influences. I enjoyed this dish during my first visit to Singapore, when it became an instant favourite.

SERVES 2

225 g (8 oz) fresh or dried thin egg noodles
225 g (8 oz) firm beancurd
300 ml (10 fl oz) oil (preferably groundnut), for deep-frying
2 teaspoons oil (preferably groundnut)
2 eggs, beaten
2 teaspoons sesame oil
½ teaspoon salt
2 tablespoons oil (preferably groundnut)

2 teaspoons chilli oil
3 tablespoons tomato purée
2 teaspoons sugar
2 tablespoons finely chopped spring onions
1 fresh chilli, seeded and shredded (optional)
2 garlic cloves, crushed
2 tablespoons light soy sauce

If you are using fresh noodles, blanch them first by boiling for 3–5 minutes in a large pan of boiling water. If you are using dried noodles, cook in boiling water for 4–5 minutes. Drain the noodles, then put into cold water until required. Cut the beancurd into 1 cm (½ in) cubes.

Heat the 300 ml (10 fl oz) of oil in a deep-fat fryer or a large wok until it almost smokes. Deep-fry the beancurd cubes for 1–2 minutes in 2 batches. When each batch of beancurd cubes is lightly browned, remove and drain well on kitchen paper.

Heat the 2 teaspoons of oil in a wok or frying-pan and add the eggs, sesame oil and salt. When cooked, the eggs should look like a thin, flat pancake. Remove from the pan, roll it up and cut in long 2.5 cm (1 in) wide strips. Set aside.

Heat a wok or large frying-pan and add the 2 tablespoons of oil. When moderately hot, add the garlic and stir-fry for 30 seconds. Quickly drain the noodles and add them to the pan with the rest of the ingredients. Continue to stir-fry the noodles until all the ingredients are well mixed. Add the egg strips and beancurd and continue to stir-fry for another 3–4 minutes.

# SPICY BLACK BEAN SAUCE NOODLES

*E*ver since I can remember, the aroma of black beans cooked with garlic has meant mouth-watering food. Because I enjoy cold noodles, I have adapted these seasonings for a light lunch dish or accompaniment for summer evening meals. The pungent sauce is cooked beforehand and allowed to cool before enlivening the cold noodles.

SERVES 2

350 g (12 oz) fresh or dried
Chinese egg noodles

Sauce

3 tablespoons oil (preferably groundnut)

2 tablespoons yellow bean sauce

2 tablespoons black beans, coarsely chopped

2 tablespoons finely chopped garlic

1 tablespoon finely chopped fresh ginger

2 tablespoons finely chopped spring onions

2 teaspoons chilli bean sauce

2 teaspoons sugar

1 tablespoon dark soy sauce

2 teaspoons chilli oil

2 tablespoons rice wine or dry sherry

150 ml (5 fl oz) chicken or vegetable stock

1 teaspoon cornflour mixed with 1 teaspoon water

If you are using fresh noodles, blanch in a large pan of boiling water for 3–5 minutes, then immerse in cold water. If you are using dried noodles, cook in boiling water for 4–5 minutes. Drain the noodles, then put into cold water until required.

For the sauce, heat a wok or large frying-pan and add the oil. When moderately hot, add the yellow bean sauce, black bean sauce, garlic, ginger and spring onions and stir-fry for 2 minutes. Then add the rest of the ingredients, except the cornflour mixture, and continue to cook for 2 minutes. Stir in the blended cornflour and bring to the boil for 30 seconds. Remove from the heat and allow the sauce to cool. Drain the noodles thoroughly in a colander and mix with the sauce. Serve at once.

# RICE DISHES

*R*ice is the staple food of most of the Far East and Asia. Unlike bread, a Western staple that plays only a secondary role in Western cookery, rice is an integral part of every meal and is eaten many times during the day. Leftover rice is stir-fried or dried to use in rice cakes, simmered in a rice porridge, or simply eaten as a snack. Like beancurd, rice combines well with other foods and flavours. Somewhat bland by itself, it readily absorbs other tastes.

# STEAMED STICKY RICE

*I*n this recipe, the rice is suffused with many seasonings which are slowly steamed along with it. This is a dish my mother used to cook for me on those days when she could not be home to prepare lunch. She would make the dish and then set it in the warm steamer, where all the ingredients would slowly marry.

SERVES 4

glutinous or short-grained rice
  to fill a measuring jug to
  450 ml (15 fl oz) level
100 g (4 oz) fresh or frozen
  peas
100 g (4 oz) button mushrooms
1 tablespoon oil (preferably
  groundnut)
1 tablespoon finely chopped
  fresh ginger

3 tablespoons finely chopped
  spring onions
2 tablespoons finely chopped
  Sichuan preserved vegetable
  (optional)
3 tablespoons rice wine or dry
  sherry
1 tablespoon oyster sauce
2 tablespoons light soy sauce

Put the rice in a large bowl, cover with water and leave to stand for 4 hours or overnight. Drain well. Set up a steamer or put a rack inside a wok or large, deep pan. Pour in about 5 cm (2 in) of water and bring it to the boil. Put the rice in a bowl and place this into the steamer or onto the rack. Cover the pan tightly, turn the heat low and steam gently for about 20 minutes.

If you are using fresh peas, blanch in a pan of boiling water for 3 minutes; drain well. Immerse in cold water to stop them from cooking. Finely slice the mushrooms.

Heat a wok or large frying-pan and add the oil. When moderately hot, add the ginger and spring onions and stir-fry for 2 minutes. Add the mushrooms and Sichuan preserved vegetables, if using, and continue to cook for 5 minutes or until most of the liquid has evaporated. Add the rice wine, oyster sauce and soy sauce and continue to cook for 2 minutes. Stir in the steamed rice and peas.

Replenish the steamer with hot water. Transfer the rice mixture into a bowl and steam for another 30 minutes over low heat. It is now ready to be served. This rice can be kept warm in the steamer, with the heat turned off, for 25 minutes. It also reheats well.

# CURRIED FRIED RICE WITH GREEN BEANS

*C*urried rice has an appealing and exotic aroma, and beans add colour and a contrast of textures. An exception to the classic rule for stir-frying rice, this cooked rice may be stir-fried immediately, without waiting for it to cool. This is a grand rice dish for any meal.

SERVES 4

2 tablespoons oil (preferably groundnut)
100 g (4 oz) French beans, trimmed and diced
long-grain rice measured to the 450 ml (15 fl oz) level in a measuring jug and cooked (page 11)
1 tablespoon finely chopped garlic

3 tablespoons finely chopped fresh coriander
grated rind of ½ lime
2 dried chillies, seeded and chopped
2 tablespoons fish sauce
2 teaspoons sugar
2 tablespoons curry paste
½ teaspoon salt

Heat a wok or large frying-pan and add the oil. When moderately hot, add the beans and stir-fry for about 2 minutes. Put in the rice and continue to stir-fry for 3 minutes. Stir in the rest of the ingredients and mix thoroughly. Turn the mixture onto a plate and serve at once.

# HONG KONG-STYLE FRIED RICE

*O*ne of the many memorable meals I have enjoyed in Hong Kong included a dish of rice, stir-fried with broccoli and eggs. I first sampled it in the company of the food critic Willie Mark.

SERVES 4

2 tablespoons oil (preferably groundnut)
225 g (8 oz) fresh broccoli
100 g (4 oz) fresh or frozen peas
1 teaspoon salt
2 tablespoons water

long-grain rice measured to the 450 ml (15 fl oz) level in a measuring jug and cooked (page 11)
2 eggs, beaten
2 teaspoons sesame oil

Separate the broccoli heads into florets. Peel the stalks if necessary, then slice. Dice the broccoli into very small pieces.

If you are using fresh peas, blanch in a small saucepan of boiling water for 2 minutes; if using frozen peas, blanch for 1 minute.

Heat a wok or large frying-pan and add the oil. When moderately hot, add the broccoli, peas and salt and stir-fry for about 1 minute, then add the water. Continue to stir-fry the mixture for about 2 minutes or until the broccoli is cooked. Add the cold cooked rice and stir-fry for 3 minutes. Then add the eggs and sesame oil and stir-fry for a further 2 minutes. Turn the mixture onto a platter and serve at once.

# THAI AROMATIC FRIED RICE

*T*hai cuisine has been influenced by the Chinese, but there is a great deal of originality in the Thai tradition. The pungent flavour of the fish sauce mellows when it is cooked, leaving a fragrant aroma. The result is an unusually piquant rice dish. You may stir-fry the cooked rice without waiting for it to cool.

SERVES 4

2 tablespoons oil (preferably groundnut)
100 g (4 oz) onion, finely chopped
long-grain rice measured to the 450 ml (15 fl oz) level in a measuring jug and cooked (page 11)
¼ teaspoon salt

1 tablespoon fish sauce
2 teaspoons chilli bean sauce
3 tablespoons tomato purée
3 tablespoons finely chopped spring onions
2 tablespoons finely chopped fresh coriander
4 eggs, beaten

Heat a wok or large frying-pan and add the oil. When moderately hot, add the onion and stir-fry for 3 minutes. Put in the rice and continue to stir-fry for another 3 minutes. Add the rest of the ingredients, except the eggs. Stir-fry the mixture for a further 5 minutes over a high heat. Next add the beaten eggs and cook for 3 minutes or until the eggs have set. Turn the mixture onto a platter and serve.

# SWEETCORN AND GINGER FRIED RICE

*S*weetcorn and rice go well together, with their contrasting and complementary textures, colours and flavours. The addition of ginger makes them a little exotic – a true East–West delight. Use fresh corn if possible, and be sure the cooked rice is cold before stir-frying. This will keep it from absorbing too much oil and becoming sticky. This economical and healthy dish may be eaten as a rice salad or vegetable accompaniment to other foods.

SERVES 4

450 g (1 lb) fresh sweetcorn on the cob, or 275 g (10 oz) tinned sweetcorn

1 tablespoon oil (preferably groundnut)

1½ tablespoons finely chopped fresh ginger

2 tablespoons finely chopped spring onions

2 tablespoons rice wine or dry sherry

long-grain rice measured to the 450 ml (15 fl oz) level in a measuring jug and cooked (page 11)

¼ teaspoon salt

¼ teaspoon freshly ground pepper

2 tablespoons sesame oil

Remove the corn kernels with a sharp knife or cleaver. You should end up with about 275 g (10 oz). If you are using tinned corn, empty the contents into a sieve, drain well and set aside.

Heat a wok or large frying-pan until hot and add the oil. Put in the ginger and spring onions and stir-fry for a few seconds. Add the rice wine and continue to stir-fry a few more seconds. Stir in the cold cooked rice and stir-fry for 5 minutes, then add the corn, salt and pepper, and continue to stir-fry for 2 minutes. Finally, add the sesame oil and stir-fry for a further 4 minutes until the corn is thoroughly cooked. Serve at once, or cold as a rice salad.

# PINEAPPLE FRIED RICE

*I* first enjoyed this unusual rice dish in Hong Kong and only subsequently learned that it is of Thai origin. Thai cooks commonly hollow out the pineapple and fill it with fried rice or some other tasty stuffing. It is a very attractive way to serve fried rice, but hollowing out the fruit takes a little effort. An easier is to cut the pineapple in half lengthways.

SERVES 4

1 fresh pineapple
25 g (1 oz) Chinese dried
   mushrooms
2 tablespoons oil (preferably
   groundnut)
1 small onion, finely chopped
100 g (4 oz) runner beans or
   French beans, trimmed and
   diced

long-grain rice measured to the
   450 ml (15 fl oz) level in a
   measuring jug and cooked
   (page 11)
2 eggs
2 tablespoons dark soy sauce
1 tablespoon fish sauce

Carefully cut off and save the pineapple top, leaving about 2.5 cm (1 in) of the pineapple under the leaves, if you want to use the whole shell for serving. Alternatively, you can cut the pineapple in half lengthways after disposing of the top and leaves. Scoop out the inside fruit, leaving the outer shell of the pineapple intact to serve the fried rice. Coarsely chop the pineapple flesh, discarding the tough centre core.

Soak the dried mushrooms in warm water for 20 minutes until soft. Squeeze out the excess liquid from the mushrooms and remove and discard the stalks. Cut the caps into small dice.

Heat a wok or large frying-pan and add the oil. When almost smoking, add the mushrooms, onion and beans and stir-fry for 1 minute. Mix in the cold cooked rice and stir-fry for 1 minute. Add the eggs, soy sauce and fish sauce and continue to stir-fry for 5 minutes over high heat. Stir in the chopped pineapple and stir-fry for about 2 minutes. Spoon the mixture into the hollowed-out pineapple shell and replace the top, or pile the mixture onto the two halves, and serve the remaining rice on a platter.

# FRAGRANT COCONUT RICE

*F*or this recipe you may use 'easy cook' rice. It is one of those rare dishes in which such pre-cooked rice works well, partly because of the richness and oils in the coconut. Unusual as the combination of spices may seem, you will find them a harmonious blend with this dish. If you use long-grain rice it will be a little sticky, as it should be. The rice reheats well but should be warmed over a very low heat.

SERVES 4

2 tablespoons oil (preferably groundnut)
175 g (6 oz) onion, finely chopped
long-grain or 'easy cook' rice measured to the 450 ml (15 fl oz) level in a measuring jug
1 teaspoon turmeric

2 teaspoons salt
450 ml (15 fl oz) tinned coconut milk
150 ml (5 fl oz) chicken or vegetable stock
2 whole cloves
1 whole cinnamon stick
2 bay leaves

Heat the oil in a large flameproof casserole until moderately hot. Add the onion and stir-fry for 2 minutes. Put in the rice, turmeric and salt, and continue to cook for 2 minutes.

Add the coconut milk and stock and bring the mixture to the boil. Stir in the whole cloves, cinnamon and bay leaves. Turn the heat as low as possible and cook the rice undisturbed for 20 minutes. It is ready to serve when the rice is cooked.

# TWO-MUSHROOM RICE

*T*his is a simple vegetarian adaptation of a traditional chicken-rice-mushroom dish my mother often made when I was a child. Even without the chicken, it remains a favourite of mine. One must properly appreciate the mushroom which, in the words of a discriminating scholar, 'belongs to that category of plants used in cooking whose main function is to add less flavour than the spices and herbs, less bulk than the real vegetables, and to absorb differentially the flavours of the dish, in order to bring out, by subtle chemistry, the highest and most delicate tastes'. Once you begin to think of mushrooms in this way and to use them accordingly, all mushroom dishes take on a special charm and flavour. Save the water in which the dried mushrooms have been soaked, as they give an additional earthy flavour to the cooked rice.

SERVES 4

25 g (1 oz) Chinese dried mushrooms

900 ml (1½ pints) very hot water

225 g (8 oz) button mushrooms

1 tablespoon oil (preferably groundnut)

3 tablespoons finely chopped spring onions

½ teaspoon salt

2 tablespoons light soy sauce

long-grain rice measured to the 450 ml (15 fl oz) level in a measuring jug

Soak the dried mushrooms in 900 ml (1½ pints) of very hot water for 20 minutes until soft. Remove them with a slotted spoon and save the liquid. Squeeze the excess liquid from the mushrooms and remove and discard the stalks. Cut the caps into quarters. Cut the button mushrooms into quarters.

Heat a wok or large frying-pan and add the oil. When hot, add the spring onion, salt and button mushrooms and stir-fry for 2 minutes. Put in the dried mushrooms and stir-fry for another minute or until all the liquid has evaporated. Remove the mixture and set aside.

Add the mushrooms, soy sauce and mushroom liquid to the rice in a pan and bring it to the boil. Continue boiling until most of the surface liquid has evaporated. This should take about 15–20 minutes. At this point, cover the pan with a very tight-fitting lid, turn the heat as low as possible and let the rice cook undisturbed with the mushrooms for 15–20 minutes.

# SINGAPORE-STYLE LETTUCE FRIED RICE

*T*his is an easy fried dish to make. The chilli adds zest and sparkle to the dish, and the lettuce provides a refreshing touch.

SERVES 4

15 g (½ oz) Chinese dried mushrooms

2 tablespoons oil (preferably groundnut)

4 shallots, sliced

3 garlic cloves, crushed

long-grain rice measured to the 450 ml (15 fl oz) level in a measuring jug and cooked (page 11)

50 g (2 oz) fresh or frozen peas

3 tablespoons finely chopped spring onions

2 fresh chillies

2 eggs, beaten

3 tablespoons light soy sauce

½ teaspoon salt

¼ teaspoon freshly ground black pepper

225 g (8 oz) iceberg lettuce, finely shredded

GARNISH

2 tablespoons finely chopped spring onions

Soak the dried mushrooms in warm water for 20 minutes until soft. Squeeze the excess liquid from the mushrooms and remove and discard the stalks. Cut the caps into small dice.

Heat a wok or large frying-pan and add the oil. When almost smoking, add the shallots and garlic and stir-fry for 30 seconds. Put in the cold cooked rice and stir-fry for 1 minute, then add the peas, spring onions and chillies and continue to stir-fry for another 3 minutes. Stir in the beaten egg, soy sauce, salt and pepper and stir-fry for a further 2 minutes or until the eggs have set.

Finally, add the lettuce and mix thoroughly. Turn the mixture onto a serving plate and garnish with the spring onions. Serve at once.

# INDEX